How to Start, Set Up and Manage Your Own Business Under President Trump's "Tax Cuts and Jobs Act of 2017"

by Donald E. Willmoth Sr.

Dorrance Publishing Co
585 Alpha Drive
Pittsburgh, PA 15238
Visit our website at *www.dorrancebookstore.com*

ISBN: 978-1-6442-6657-1
eISBN: 978-1-4809-8666-4

My special thanks to the staff of AFTE for helping me make this book possible, I thank:

Donald E. Willmoth Jr

Bridget M. Farrell

Alicia K. Willmoth

Wendy S. Lamkin

Yuliana Basurto

Table of Contents

PREFACE

This book is intended to show a potential business owner how to start, set up, and manage their own business. I have helped many people achieve their dream of going into business for themselves and succeeding. If you are self-motivated, self-disciplined, and have a passion to succeed, you can.

I started my own business 40 years ago with an initial investment of $600. With a lot of hard work and dedication, I now have one of the most successful financial services in the United States.

You, too, can succeed in starting your own business by following the blueprint that I have written for you in this book.

Having your own business can be very challenging, but it can also be most rewarding. Being your own boss can be very empowering.

The good news, thanks to the new tax law, Tax Cuts and Jobs Act of 2017, people aspiring to go into business for themselves has never been better. This act eliminates several regulations that have been stifling business growth for many years. The act also greatly lowers federal income taxes on businesses. The business economic climate is the best it has been in years to start your own business.

To summarize, this book gives the person starting their own business an outline, if followed, greatly enhances their chances of succeeding in their own business.

I can't guarantee that in reading this book you will succeed, but by following the information that I have outlined in this book, you will have a much better chance of succeeding!

TAX CUTS AND JOBS ACT OF 2017

The New Pass-Through Deduction: How Small Businesses Will Pay Less Income Taxes.
The new tax code (IRC Sec 199A) contains a 20% deduction of business profits for pass-through businesses, sole proprietorship, partnerships, LLC's, and S corporations.

Here's how it works:
The pass-through is how sole proprietorships, partnerships, LLC's, and S corporations are taxed. The business's profits or losses are passed through on to each owner's tax return. The owners then pay personal income tax onto their share of the profit or loss.

The new tax law allows small business owners to reduce their taxable business profit income by 20%. For example, a sole proprietor making $100,000 profit will receive a $20,000 deduction and only pay income taxes on $80,000 business profit.

100% Bonus Depreciation
Bonus Depreciation allows a business owner to deduct a substantial amount of a long-term asset's cost in a single year instead of depreciating the cost over many years. The TCJA increases the bonus depreciation amount to 100% that can be deducted the first year. The increase goes into effect for long-term assets placed in service after September

27th, 2017. In addition, for the first time, bonus depreciation may be applied for the purchases of used, as well as new, property.

Under the new tax act, the corporate tax rate will fall from 39% to 21%. This is a flat rate on all profits. This is permanent.

Also, the corporate Alternative Minimum Tax will be eliminated.

The decision to open your own business

Why do you want to start a business? Is it money, freedom, and flexibility or some other reason? What are your skills? You must be very familiar with the products or services you will provide.

How much capital will you need to start your business?

You need to plan, set goals, and above all, know yourself. What are your strengths? What are your weaknesses?

Three vital characteristics of going into business for yourself is that you must be very disciplined, self-motivated, and have a passion to succeed.

Your business will dominate your life. Are you ready to make this sacrifice?

What do you want from life, not just what you want from your business?

Do you have the support of your family?

Who will buy your products or services?

Who will be your competition?

Evaluate your target market, customers/clients. Do a market analysis.

Determine your form of business: Proprietorship, Partnership, C Corporation, or S Corporation, etc.

Nothing happens in business until a sale is made! You will wear many hats as a business owner, but the most important hat that you will wear will be that as a salesperson. Even as a medical doctor or candle stick maker, you must convince whoever you are in front of to purchase what you are selling!

It is to be noted if you take good care of your customers/clients, you will make money, which is your ultimate goal.

How to choose your business name

It is best to pick a name that tells what you do. For example, Jose's Mexican Restaurant tells what it is. You can find the right business name with creativity and market research.

How to pick your business location

You have heard it said that when you are looking for a place to do business, the most important consideration is location, location, location. Your business location determines the taxes, zoning laws, and regulations your business will be subject to. You'll need to make a strategic decision about which state, city, and neighborhood you choose to start your business in.

Where you locate your business depends on the location of your target market and your personal preferences. In addition, you should consider the costs, benefits, and restrictions of different government agencies.

Location can be critical if you are in a retail business. So, don't sacrifice location for low rent costs.

Price: Can you afford where you want to be?

Access to parking or public transportation: Can people find you?

Competition: Are your competitors close to you?

Local, city, and state rules and regulations: Investigate the regulations.

How to choose your business structure

The business structure you choose influences everything from day-to-day operations, to taxes, to what assets you need to purchase. You should choose a business structure that gives you the right balance of legal protections and benefits.

Your business structure affects how much you pay in taxes, your ability to raise money, the paperwork you need to file, and your personal liability.

You'll need to choose a business structure before you register your business. Most businesses will also need to get federal and state ID number and file in the appropriate license and permits.

While you may convert to a different business structure in the future, there may be restrictions based on your location. This could also result in tax consequences, among other complications. Consulting with business counselors, attorneys, and accountants can prove helpful.

Sole proprietorship

A sole proprietorship is easiest to form and gives you complete control of your business. Sole proprietorships are not separate business entities. Your profit or loss goes onto your personal tax return. Also, your business assets and liabilities are not separate from your personal assets and liabilities. You can be held personally liable for the debts and obligations of the business.

Banks are hesitant to lend money to sole proprietorships.

It is to be noted that most businesses start as sole proprietors.

Partnership

Partnerships are the simplest structure for two or more people to own a business together. Partnerships can be a good choice for businesses with multiple owners, professional groups (e.g. attorneys).

Partnerships are not separate business entities. Your profit or loss goes onto the partner's personal tax return. Also, your business assets and liabilities are not separate from your personal assets and liabilities. Partners can be held personally liable for the debts and obligations of the partnership.

C corporation

A corporation, sometimes called a C corp, is a legal entity that's separate from its owners. Corporations can make a profit, are taxed, and can be held legally liable.

Corporations offer the strongest protection to its owners from personal liability, but the cost to form a corporation is higher than other structures. Corporations also require more extensive record keeping, operational processes, and reporting.

Corporations pay income tax on their profits.

Corporations can be a good choice for medium or higher-risk businesses, businesses that need to raise money, and businesses that plan to "go public" or eventually be sold.

S corporation

An S corporation is a special type of corporation. S corps allow profits and some losses to be passed through directly to owner's personal tax return.

Not all states tax S corps equally, but most recognize them the same way the federal government does and taxes the shareholders accordingly. Some states tax S corps on profits above a specified limit, and other states don't recognize the S corp election at all, simply treating the business as a C corp. Check with your state how the taxes are handled.

To create an S Corp, you will need to file IRS form 2553 with the IRS within 90 days after you incorporate.

There are special limits on S corps. S corps can't have more than 100 shareholders, and all shareholders must be U.S. citizens. You'll also still have to follow strict filling and operational process of a C Corp.

S Corps also have an independent life, just like C Corps, if a shareholder leaves the company or sells his or her shares, the S Corp can continue doing business relatively undisturbed.

Limited liability company (LLC)

A Limited liability company (LLC) can take the form of a sole proprietor, partnership, C Corporation, or an S Corporation. You must make this determination when you set your company up.

LLC's protect you from personal liability in most instances. Your personal assets, like your vehicle, house, and savings accounts, won't be at risk in case your LLC faces bankruptcy or lawsuits.

Profits and losses can get passed through to your personal tax return income except for C corps. However, members of an LLC are considered self-employed and must pay self-employment tax contributions towards Medicare and Social Security.

LLC's can have a limited life in many states. When a member joins or leaves an LLC, some states may require the LLC to be dissolved and re-formed with new membership, unless there's already an agreement in place within the LLC for buying, selling, and transferring ownership.

LLC's can be a good choice for medium or higher risk businesses, owners with significant personal assets they want to be protected, and owners who want to pay a lower tax rate than they would as a corporation.

Nonprofit corporation

Nonprofit corporations are organized to do charity, education, religious, literary, or scientific work. Because their work benefits the public, nonprofits can receive tax-exempt status, meaning they don't pay state or federal income taxes on any profits it makes.

Nonprofits must file with the IRS to get tax exemption. Nonprofits are often called 501 (c)(3) corporations, a reference to the section of the Internal Revenue Code that is most commonly used to grant tax-exempt status.

Nonprofit corporations need to follow organizational rules very similar to regular C corp. They need to follow special rules about what they do with any profits they earn. For example, they can't distribute profits to members or political campaigns.

How to register your business name to protect it

Choose a business name that reflects what your business does. Once you settle on a name you like, you need to protect it. There are different ways to register your business name. Each way of registering your name serves a different purpose, and some may be legally required depending on your business structure and location.

Doing Business As (DBA) name

You need to register your DBA, also known as a trade name, fictitious name, or assumed name with the state, county, or city your business is located in. Registering your DBA name doesn't provide legal protection by itself, but most states require you to register your DBA to do business in their state. Some business structures require you to use a DBA.

Even if you're not required to register a DBA, you might want to anyway. A DBA lets you conduct business under a different identity from your own personal name or your formal business entity name. As a bonus, getting a DBA and federal tax ID numbers (EIN) allows you to open a business bank account. The IRS prefers you to keep your business income and expenses separate from your personal income and expenses

Determine your DBA requirements based on your specific location. Requirements vary by business structure as well as by state, county, and municipality, so check with local government offices and websites.

Partnership: To register a partnership, you must get a federal ID, number (EIN) from the IRS to file your partnership tax return (Form 1065).

Entity name: C corporation, S corporation You must register with your state to get the articles of incorporation. And you must also have a federal ID number from the IRS to do your corporate income tax reporting.

An entity name can protect the name of your business at a state level. Your entity name is how the state identifies your business. Each state may have different rules about what your entity name can be and usage of company suffixes. Most states don't allow you to register a name that's already been registered by someone else, and some states require your entity name to reflect the kind of business it represents.

In most cases, your entity name registration protects your business and prevents anyone else in the state from operating under the same entity name.

Domain name

If you want an online presence for your business, start by registering a domain name, also known as your website address or URL.

Once you register your domain name, no one else can use it for as long as you continue to own it. It's a good way to protect your brand presence online.

You'll register your domain name through a registrar service. Consult a directory of accredited registrars to determine which ones are safe to use and then pick one that offers you the best combination of price and customer service. You'll need to renew your domain registration on a regular basis.

How to calculate your startup costs

How much money will it take to start your business? You will need to calculate the startup costs.

One of the keys of successful business is preparation. Before your business opens its doors, you'll have bills to pay. Understanding your expenses will help you launch successfully.

Identify your startup and one time expenses

Most business fall into one of three categories: brick-and-mortar businesses, online businesses, and service providers. You'll face different startup expenses depending on your business type. There are common startup costs you're likely to have no matter what. Look through this list, and make sure to add any other expenses that are unique to your business.

- Office expenses
- Equipment
- Licenses and permits
- Insurance
- Employee salaries
- Advertising and marketing
- Market research
- Printed marketing materials
- Professional fees

- Rent
- Utilities

Once you have your list of expenses, you can estimate how much they'll cost. This process will be different for each expense you have.

After you've identified your business expenses and how much they'll cost, you should organize your expenses into one-time expenses and monthly expenses.

One-time expenses are the initial costs needed to start the business. Buying major equipment, hiring a logo designer, and paying for permits, licenses, and fees are generally considered to be one-time expenses. Make sure to keep track of your expenses for your accountant when it's time to file your taxes

Typical monthly business expenses

Accounting	Interest	Professional assistance
Advertising	Laundry	Outside help
Auto/Truck	Legal	Postage
Bad debts	Licenses/Permits	Rent
Bank charges	Maintenance/Repairs	Security
Credit cards	Materials	Shop
Freight	Office	Supplies
Insurance	Parts	Taxes – Payroll, property
Telephone	Tools	Travel
Uniforms	Utilities	

It is to be noted that mileage expenses generally exceed the actual auto expenses. The standard mileage rate has averaged 54.9 cents per mile from years 2015-2018.

Typical monthly cash flow statement

Essentially, the monthly cash flow statement is concerned with the flow of cash in and out of the business.

Monthly Income $ _______________

Monthly Expenses:

Advertising $ _______________
Auto (mileage) $ _______________
Bank fees $ _______________
Delivery $ _______________
Maintenance/
Repairs $ _______________
Miscellaneous $ _______________
Office $ _______________
Professional $ _______________
Rent $ _______________
Supplies $ _______________
Taxes $ _______________
Telephone $ _______________
Utilities $ _______________
Total monthly expenses $ _______________
Total cash flow (Income minus expenses) $ _______________

Typical monthly budget report

A budget is a financial plan for a defined period, usually a year.

Income	Monthly budget	Actual amount	Difference
Income:	$ _________	$ _________	$ _________
Expenses:			
Advertising	$ _________	$ _________	$ _________
Auto	$ _________	$ _________	$ _________
Bank fees	$ _________	$ _________	$ _________
Delivery	$ _________	$ _________	$ _________
Maintenance	$ _________	$ _________	$ _________
Office	$ _________	$ _________	$ _________
Professional	$ _________	$ _________	$ _________
Rent	$ _________	$ _________	$ _________
Supplies	$ _________	$ _________	$ _________
Taxes	$ _________	$ _________	$ _________
Telephone	$ _________	$ _________	$ _________
Utilities	$ _________	$ _________	$ _________
Total expenses	$ _________	$ _________	$ _________
Net income	$ _________	$ _________	$ _________

(Income minus expenses)

How to open a business bank/ credit union account

A business bank account helps you stay legally compliant and protected. It also provides benefits to your customers and employees. The IRS prefers you to keep your business expenses and income separate from your personal expenses and income.

Benefits of business bank accounts

Common business accounts include a checking account, savings account, credit card account, and a merchant services account. Merchant services accounts allow you to accept credit and debit card transactions from your customers. You can open a business bank account once you've gotten your federal EIN or a DBA.

Documents you need to open a business bank account

Once you've picked your bank, here are some of the most common documents banks ask for when you open a business bank account. Some banks may ask for more.

Employer Identification Number (EIN) (or a Social Security number, if you're a sole proprietorship)

Your business's formation documents (Articles of incorporation, if C or S Corp)

Ownership agreements (DBA) assumed names certificate

How to fund your business

Funding your business is one of the first and most important financial choices most business owners make. How you choose to fund your business could affect how you structure and run your business.

Self-funding your business (The most common)

Most of small-business are self-funded. Self-funding can come in the form of turning to family and friends for capital or using your savings accounts.

With self-funding, you retain complete control over the business, but you also take on all the risk yourself. Be careful not to spend more than you can afford and be especially careful if you choose to use tap into retirement accounts early. Be aware of tapping into a retirement account, you are taxed by the IRS. If you are under the age of 59 ½, you will pay a 10% penalty, plus the tax on the tax bracket that you are in.

How to get a small business bank or credit union loan

You need to determine the size of your loan. Then you need to determine if you can afford it.

Banks and credit unions will need the following information to open an account:

- Personal tax returns

- Legal documents (such as articles of incorporation or DBA (assumed name certificate)
- Contact banks or credit unions to request a loan. You will want to compare offers to get the best possible terms for your loan.

How to apply for an SBA loan

SBA loans are popular for existing businesses in need of working capital. They're also an option for many startups looking to finance the beginning or purchase of a business. SBA loans are difficult to qualify for, generally needing a 680+ credit score, a strong financial history, and possibly some collateral. For this reason, it's more challenging for a startup to get an SBA loan.

SBA loans are also among the cheapest loans you can get with lower interest rates and longer terms than other forms of financing. However, SBA lenders will typically require a down payment of 20-30% of the total startup costs. Many people use their 401(k), IRA, or ROBS for their down payment for an SBA loan.

HOW TO USE AN IRA/401(k) TO START OR BUY A BUSINESS

A Rollover for Business Startups (ROBS) allows you to use savings in your 401(k) or IRA to fund your startup or to buy a business without any penalties or immediate tax obligations.

How to set up a ROBS

To set up a ROBS, you must form a C corporation and then establish a 401(k) for that company. Next, you roll over funds from your personal 401(k) or IRA into the new company's retirement plan. Using the funds you've just rolled over, the new 401(k) plan buys stock in the new C corp. With that, your startup is funded!

You can also use a ROBS for a business acquisition, working capital, or as a down payment for additional financing.

You will be an employee at the highest level of your new corporation.

As a trustee of your new 401(k) plan, you direct the plan to purchase stock in your new corporation, therefore providing your business with the funding needs.

The ROBS isn't a loan or withdrawal but is instead a way to tap into your retirement funds before retirement age.

There is no requirement to repay the money, even if your business fails.

Who a ROBS is right for?

You plan to work full-time in the business

You have enough retirement money in your IRA or 401(k) to start or buy a business.

Assets and equipment

Your business will need assets and equipment. Figure out which assets you need, and how to pay for them. The assets you need will depend upon the nature of your business.

Assets, like buildings, vehicles, and equipment, are used for regular business activity and lose value over time. Things like printer paper, which get used up, typically don't get counted as assets. Once you've determined all the assets you need for your business, you can decide how to acquire them.

How to buy assets

Buying equipment can be a good option if you have enough cash or credit available and you're confident you'll be using the assets for a long time.

Buying benefits:

- The lifetime cost to buy is usually less than leasing
- Assets look good on your balance sheet. They increase your net worth
- You can depreciate the entire cost of the asset, new or used, without having to come up with any cash outlay
- Lending institutions look at your business assets to loan you money.

Buying disadvantages:

- Need more cash or credit upfront
- Less opportunity to "test out" the asset
- You could be fully liable for maintenance and replacement

Buy with cash or credit

If you buy your assets with cash, you'll own it in full right away. But it also means you'll have less cash available to cover operating expenses.

How to lease assets

Leasing can be a good option if you need to quickly get a lot of equipment or if the equipment you need is very expensive. Commercial space is usually leased, so you can lease a place to run your business. In some cases, leasing can be less expensive than purchasing with a high-interest loan.

Leasing benefits:
- Need less cash or credit upfront
- Leases let you test out the equipment
- Maintenance is sometimes included at no extra cost
- Lease payments for business assets are tax deductible

Leasing disadvantages:
- The lifetime cost is normally higher than buying
- Replacing it when the lease is up could be expensive
- You can't depreciate leased assets

Every lease can be structured differently, so investigate the details of your offer to make sure you're getting something that works for you.

How to get federal and state tax ID numbers

Your state tax ID and federal tax ID numbers, also known as an employer identification number (EIN), work like a personal social security number but for your business. They enable your business to pay state and federal taxes.

To get your federal ID number (EIN) go to www.IRS.gov
Your business needs a federal tax ID number if it does any of the following:

- Files tax returns
- Pays federal tax returns
- Pays employees
- Operates as a corporation (C or S), or partnership
- Files tax returns for employment, excise, alcohol, tobacco, or firearms
- Open bank accounts
- Apply for business licenses and permits

To get state ID number, go to the state's website.
Tax obligations differ at the state and local levels, check with your state's websites.

To know whether you need a state tax ID, research and understand your state's laws regarding income taxes, and employment taxes, the two most common forms of state taxes for businesses.

The process to get a state tax ID number is like getting a federal tax ID number. You'll have to check with your state government for specific steps.

How to apply for licenses and permits

Most businesses need a combination of licenses and permits from both federal and state agencies. The requirements and fees vary based on your business activities, location, and government rules.

Federal licenses and permits

You need to get a federal license or permit if your business activities are regulated by a federal agency.

Check with the right federal agency to see how to apply.

Requirements and fees depend on your business activity and the agency issuing the license or permit. It's best to check with the issuing agency for details on the business license cost.

State licenses and permits

The licenses and permits you need from the state, county, or city will depend on the nature of your business activities and business location. Your business license fees will also vary.

States tend to regulate a broader range of activities than the federal government. For example, business activities that are commonly regulated locally include auctions, construction, and dry cleaning, farming, plumbing, restaurants, retail, and vending machines.

Some licenses and permits expire after a set period. Keep close track of when you need to renew them; it's often easier to renew than it is to apply for a new one.

Sales tax certificate: Go to salestaxstatepermit.com to get sales tax permit. Some states have no sales tax.

You'll have to research your state, county, and city regulations. Industry requirements often vary by state. Visit your state's website to find out which permits and licenses you need.

How to maintain licenses, permits, and re-certification

The documents for staying legally compliant vary based on your industry and location.

Maintain any licenses, permits, or certificates your business received from your state, city, or county. Renewal requirements vary, so it's best to check with local business licensing offices.

For example, most restaurants need to regularly renew health and safety certificates. Businesses that sell regulated items, like tobacco, alcohol, or tires, might need to regularly renew their sales permits. For professional services, like insurance agents, plumbers, or nurses, the state might require certification with a third-party board to keep your license.

For licenses, permits to sell real estate, check with the issuing institution to confirm renewal requirements for your business.

How to pay federal, state, and local taxes

Your business will need to meet its federal, state, and local tax obligations to stay in good legal standing. Your business structure and location will influence which taxes your business has to pay.

Your business is legally required to pay taxes and keep accounting records. Most businesses choose their tax year to be the same as the calendar year. You can choose a fiscal tax year if you want your 12-month accounting cycle to end in a month that isn't December.

The following are types of business taxes due:

- Federal and state income tax- Contact your state on how to pay state income tax. Seven states have no state income tax: Alaska, Florida, Nevada, South Dakota, Texas, Washington, and Wyoming.
- Self-employment tax- Sole proprietors, some partnerships, and some LLC's pay self-employment taxes, which are generated from schedule "C" from your personal tax return and from a K1 on your partnership tax return.
- Estimated tax- These payments are made quarterly for the federal and state tax returns.
- Employer tax- If your business has employees, you will be required to withhold taxes from their paychecks. Federal employment taxes include income tax, Social Security, Medicare, unemployment, and self-employment taxes.

The easiest and most economical way to file your payroll reports is to use a payroll service, such as ADP or Paychex. ADP provides customized payroll solutions for all sized businesses. It offers multiple options for paying your employees, including electronic pay cards. With this system, you can integrate payroll functions with ADP's human resources management, benefits administration, and time and attendance solutions.

- Excise tax- Contact your state on how to comply.
- Franchise tax- Some states have a franchise tax for corporations (C corps and S corps) or LLC's that operate within their border. Formulas vary by state. Check to see if your state has such a tax.

Ongoing filling requirements

Make sure that you meet all federal and state tax obligations, including income and employer taxes.

If your business had any federal licenses, permits, or certificates, you'll need to keep those up to date.

Business insurance

Business insurance protects you from the unexpected costs of running a business. Accidents, natural disasters, and lawsuits could run you out of business if you're not protected with the right insurance.

The protections you get from choosing a business structure, like an LLC or a corporation, typically only protect your personal property from lawsuits, and even that protection is limited.

Business insurance can fill in the gaps to make sure both your personal assets and your business assets are fully protected from unexpected catastrophes.

In some instances, you might be legally required to purchase certain types of business insurance.

>**Assess your risks.** Think about what kind of accidents, natural disasters, or lawsuits could damage your business. If you need help, the National Federation of Independent Businesses (NFIB) provides information for choosing insurance to help you assess your risks and to make sure you've insured every aspect of your business.
>
>**Find a reputable licensed agent.** Commercial insurance agents can help you find policies that match your business needs. They receive commissions from insurance companies when they sell policies, so it's important to find a licensed agent

that's interested in your needs as much as his/her own.

Shop around. Prices and benefits can vary significantly. You should compare rates, terms, and benefits for insurance offers from several different agents.

Re-assess every year. As your business grows, so do your liabilities. If you have purchased or replaced equipment or expanded operations, you should contact your insurance agent to discuss changes in your business and how they affect your coverage.

Marketing and Sales

Nothing happens in any business unless something is sold. *You will wear many hats in your business, but the most important hat will be your sales hat.*

Marketing takes time, money, and preparation. One of the best ways to stay on schedule and on budget is to make a marketing plan. It describes the actions you'll take to persuade potential customers to buy your products or services.

Most marketing plans covers the following topics.

Target market

Describe your customers/clients in detail. Look at the market's size, demographics, unique traits, and trends that relate to demand for your business.

Competitive advantage

Describe what gives your product or service an advantage over the competition. It might be a better product, a lower price, or an excellent customer experience. Sometimes, an environmentally friendly certification or "made in the USA" on your label can be an important factor for customers.

Sales plan

Describe how you'll sell your service or product to your customers.

List the sales methods you'll use, like retail, wholesale, or your own online store.

Marketing and sales goals

Describe your marketing and sales goals for the next year. Common marketing and sales goals are to increase email subscribers, grow market share, or increase sales by a certain percent.

Marketing action plan

Describe how you'll achieve your marketing and sales goals. List marketing channels you'll use, like online advertising, radio ads, billboards, or telemarketing. Explain your pricing strategy and how you'll use promotions.

Budget

Include a complete breakdown of the costs of your marketing plan. Try to be as accurate as possible. You'll want to keep tracking your costs once you put your plan into action. Follow the budget format that I have provided for you in this book.

Market research and competitive analysis

Market research helps you find customers for your business. Competitive analysis helps you make your business unique. Combine them to find a competitive advantage for your business.

Market research blends consumer behavior and economic trends to confirm and improve your business idea.

It's crucial to understand your consumer/client base from the outset. Market research lets you reduce risks.

Gather demographic information to better understand opportunities and limitations for gaining customers/clients. This could include population data on age, wealth, family, interests, or anything else that's relevant for your business.

Then answer these questions to get a good sense of your market.

- Demand: Is there a desire for your product or service?
- Market size: How many people would be interested in your products/services?
- Economic indicators: What is the income range and employment rate?
- Location: Where do your customers live and where can your business reach?
- Market saturation: How many similar options are already available to consumers?
- Pricing: What do potential customers/clients pay for these alternatives?

How to get free business data and trends

There are many reliable sources that provide customer and market information at no cost. Free statistics are readily available to help prospective business owners.

Consider these types of business statistics in your market research and competitive analysis:

Focus   General business statistics
Goal   Find statistics on industries, business conditions
Reference NAICS, Fed Stats, Statistical Abstract of the United States, U.S. Census Bureau

Focus   Consumer statistics
Goal   Gain info on potential customers, consumer markets
Reference Consumer Credit Data, Consumer Product Safety

Focus   Demographics
Goal   Segment the population for targeting customers
Reference American Factfinders, Bureau of Labor Statistics

Focus   Economic indicators
Goal   Know unemployment rates, loans granted and more
Reference Consumer Price Index, Bureau of Economic Analysis

Focus	Production and sales statistics
Goal	Understand demand, costs and consumer spending
Reference	Consumer Spending, Gross Domestic Product (GDP)

How to get accounting help

You will want to get help with your accounting, bookkeeping. Consider hiring a certified public accountant (CPA), bookkeeper, or using an online service.

A CPA will typically cost more than a bookkeeper or an online service. A CPA and bookkeeper can do tax returns, personal and business, and other federal and state reports.

Another solution is QuickBooks. Several businesses use Quick-Books to keep record of their income and expenses of doing business. QuickBooks products are geared mainly toward small and medium sized businesses and offer on-premises accounting applications, as well as cloud-based versions that accept business payments, manage and pay bills, and payroll functions.

How to hire and manage employees/contractors
Establish a basic payroll set up for employees/contractors. Then, manage employees/contractors properly with a general understanding of state and federal labor laws.

How to hire and pay employees/contractors
Create a plan for paying employees. Follow these steps to set up your payroll:

- Get an Employer Identification Number (EIN)
- Find out whether you need state or local tax IDs

- Decide if you want an independent contractor or an employee
- Get the employees and independent contractors name, address, and social security number.
- Ensure new employees return a completed W-4 form
- Schedule pay periods to coordinate tax withholding for IRS and state
- Create a compensation plan for holiday, vacation and leave
- Choose an in-house or external service for administering payroll
- Decide who will manage your payroll system: CPA, bookkeeper, ADP, Paycheck, etc.
- Know which records must stay on file and for how long (see record retention for businesses in this book)
- Report payroll taxes as needed on quarterly and annual basis

Employees and independent contractors

Distinguishing between employees and independent contractors can impact your bottom line, as this affects how you withhold taxes and avoids costly legal consequences. Learn the differences before hiring your first employees/contractors.

An independent contractor operates under a separate business name from your company and invoices for work completed. The key word the government uses, federal or state to determine if the person is an employee or contractor, is how much *control* you have over the contractor.

Independent contractors can sometimes qualify as employees in a legal sense. The Equal Employment Opportunity Commission created a guide for making the determination.

If your contractor is discovered to meet the legal definition of employee, you may need to pay back taxes and penalties, provide benefits, and reimburse for wages stipulated under the Fair Labor Standards Act.

You must issue a W-2 for employees. You must also issue an IRS form 1099 Misc. for contractors making $600 or more.

Required employee benefits

- Social Security taxes: Employers must pay Social Security taxes at the same rate as their employees.
- Workers' Compensation: Required through a commercial carrier, self-insured basis, or state Workers' Compensation Program.
- Disability Insurance: Disability pay is required in California, Hawaii, New Jersey, New York, Rhode Island, and Puerto Rico.
- Leave benefits: Most leave benefits are optional outside those stipulated in the Family and Medical Leave Act (FMLA).
- Unemployment insurance: Varies by state, and you may need to register with your state workforce agency.

Follow federal and state labor laws

Protect workers' rights and your business by adhering to labor laws, which means you must ensure that business practices align with industry regulations.

Consult the Department of Labor's federal and state law resources.

How to build a business website

You must have a web presence. Consumers turn to the internet for everything, from product research to location and operating hours. Having even a simple website that's well-designed can give you an edge in your business, and if you have products/services to sell, your site can open new markets and expand your business cheaply and easily.

The following is a step-by step guide to creating a successful business website.

1. **Determine the primary purpose of your website**

    A business website generally serves as a space to provide general information about your company or a direct platform for e-commerce. Regardless of whether you create a simple website that tells a little about your company or a more complex e-commerce site, the most important thing you must do is say on the home page, in plain terms, what your company does.

2. **Decide your domain name**

    Your domain name is one of the most important features of your website. It's the URL you'll be sharing with your current and potential clients and promoting on social media. Therefore, you want it to be descriptive and easy to remember and type in. Try to keep it short and steer clear of abbreviations, acronyms, and numbers, if possible, to avoid customer confusion.

You also need to decide your top-level domain or TLD. This is the suffix at the end of your domain name, such as .com, .net, .biz, or .org. Once you've selected your domain name, you'll need to confirm its availability and purchase it through a domain registrar, like GoDaddy, Squarespace, Wix, or Web.com.

3. **How to choose a web host**

   Every website needs a "host," a server where all the data is stored for the public to access at all times. As a business, hosting your own website is simply too large of an expense, so you'll need to select an external host.

4. **How to build your pages**

   A good website is more than a static home page. You'll want to create pages dedicated to different aspects of your business, such as a detailed catalog of your products or services or a blog section for company updates. As for your overall website, you want to be sure each page supports the primary goal of the website, has a clear purpose, and includes a call to action (e.g. learn more, sign up, contact us, or buy this).

A contact page, your customers direct link to you, is one of the most important sections of a website, so make sure you include as much information as you can (phone number, email address, and physical location, if applicable).

If your business doesn't already have a logo, hire a graphic designer or create a logo yourself to use on your website. This will help your clients identify your company quickly and easily on the web.

Vistaprint (vistaprint.com) does a good job in helping you create a logo, business cards, and brochures.

Be clear about what your business does. Explain what your business does in a clear, concise statement and lead with that. Visitors should be able to understand what you do within seconds of landing on your home page.

Social media for a business

If you aren't using social media as a small business owner, you are missing out on a valuable and inexpensive marketing tool. With about 70% of Americans using social media, your social media marketing campaigns have the potential to reach a lot of people.

"Social media provides targeting capability, as well as reach and scale, at a lower cost than almost all other marketing channels."

It's important for you to invest in the platforms where you're more likely to reach and engage with your customers/clients.

To choose the best social media channels for you to interact with your customers, take some time to familiarize yourself with each network, how it runs, and what demographics use that platform.

The following are the basics you need to know about today's most popular social media platforms.

Facebook

Facebook is the biggest social network on the web, both in name recognition and total number of users. With billions of active users, Facebook is a great medium for connecting people from all over the world with your business.

Considering that Facebook has a wealth of options for any type of organization, it's a great starting point for your business, regardless of your industry. You can use Facebook to share photos, videos, important company updates, and more. Additionally, the site can be lower-maintenance than other social networks. Whether you post several updates a day or only a few a week, will aid you in your marketing effort.

Twitter

With Twitter, you can share short text updates (240 characters or fewer), videos, images, links, polls, and more. You can also easily interact with other users by mentioning their usernames in your posts, so Twitter is a great way to quickly connect with people all around the world.

Twitter averages millions of active users worldwide and is one of the top ten websites in the United States. Because of its wide reach, this platform is not only a great way to market your business, but also an effective channel for handling customer service. For example, if you maintain an active Twitter presence, customers who are also active on the platform will seek you out to express concerns or share their praise.

Snapchat

Snapchat is another mobile-only visual social media network that's known for its disappearing content. The more than 300 million monthly app users can send videos and photos, available for up to ten seconds at a time to one another, or post content to their public stories, which disappears after 24 hours. During the past five years, the app has expanded to include chat, messaging, image storage, events, and media content. Now content can easily be saved and uploaded elsewhere.

Because posts are so temporary, there is less pressure to create super-polished content. You can also see how many and which specific users viewed your story. A business will mostly likely utilize the platform's stories feature, but keep in mind that only users who have added you can view your stories content. However, once you have an audience, stories allow you to easily create story-driven and inter-active content.

YouTube

YouTube is a video-sharing platform with more than one billion users where people can view, upload, rate, share, and comment on content. Now owned by Google, the site is a huge hub for news and entertainment.

How to write a business plan

A business plan is a formal statement of business goals, reasons that are attainable, and plans for reaching them.

Free Business Plan Templates for Startups
Writing a business plan is one of the most crucial elements of starting a business. However, it doesn't have to be the most frustrating. Here are 12 free business plan templates. These templates will outline the steps you need to do to write a business plan.

1. **The Balance**

   The Balance business plan template is broken into sections, such as executive summary, business overview, market analysis and competition, and sales and marketing plan. The Balance also offers a step-by-step guide to writing a business plan to go with the template. Each section can be copied into a Word, Excel, or similar Office document.

2. **Bplans**

   Bplans offers a free Word business plan template complete with instructions and a table of contents. It also offers many standard business plan sections, such as executive summary, company summary, and products and services. Once you register, you can download the materials and choose from a wide variety of businesses in different industries. Whether your business is online, service-based or a food establishment, Bplans's Word business plan templates are comprehensive and great for beginners or new business owners.

3. **FormSwift**

    Formswift has a collection of over 500 document templates, including a business plan template. You can fill out the template with the help of a step-by-step guide and then export it into Word or a PDF for later use.

4. **Office Depot Business Resource Center**

    Office Depot Business Resource Center contains free business plan samples for retailers, manufacturers, and service providers. There are five total documents available with two in rich text format (RTF) that is suitable for most word processing programs and one file that requires Microsoft Word 6.0 or above. The other two files are Microsoft Excel spreadsheets that are compatible with Excel 4.0 and above.

5. **Rocket Lawyer**

    With Rocket Lawyer business plan template, not only do you create a free business plan, but you also get the advantage of an attorney's advice to make sure your document is legally sound. The questionnaire-style template asks for key information about your business, such as founders, structure, marketing plans, and financial projections. Your completed document is available for download as a word document for free with a one-week trial subscription.

How to buy an existing business

In buying an existing business, the buyer typically takes over full ownership of the business. The largest advantage is having an existing blueprint that can include important factors, like an established customer base, defined operating expenses, and fully trained employees. When you buy an existing business, you also get complete control over its direction.

The challenge for you, the buyer, is to formulate a valuation that is accurate and will prove to provide you with an acceptable return on your investment.

The following is information that you need to determine whether you should buy a business or not.

- Analyze tax returns from the past three years (business and personal).
- Is the business profitable? Have the sales gone up or down in three years?
- List of assets.
- Liabilities of the business.
- Why is the owner selling the business?
- How are you going purchase the business, owner finance, or borrowing the money?
- How much was paid to the owners, etc. in discretionary earnings?

How to calculate the value of a business:

There are many different methods to determine a fair price for the sale of the business. Here are a few:

> **Assets minus liabilities method:** To arrive at this amount, subtract the assets from the liabilities on the business financial statement.
>
> **Market value:** The market value compares your business to similar businesses that have already sold.
>
> **Multiple method value:** Is clearly the best way to go. The business sells for "X" times the yearly earnings. This is how much money you can expect to make from the business.
>
> **Owner benefit method:** The pre-tax profit + owner's salary + additional owner perks + interest + depreciation less allocation for capital expenditures.

The theory behind the owner benefit number is to take the business's profits, plus the owner's salary and benefits and to add back the non-cash expenses. History has shown that this methodology, while not bulletproof, is the most effective way to establish the valuation basis of business. Then, a multiple, based upon a variety of factors, is applied to this number and a valuation is established.

How to buy a franchise

A franchise is a business where one business owner (the "franchiser") sells the rights to their business logo, name, and model to an independent entrepreneur (the "franchisee"). Restaurants, hotels, and service-oriented businesses are commonly franchised.

When you buy a franchise, you get the right to use the name, logo, and products of a larger brand. You'll also get to benefit from brand recognition, promotions, and marketing. But it also means you must follow rules from the larger brand about how you run your business.

Starting a business from scratch can be challenging.

Franchising gives you more guidance but less control.

Once you've found a franchise or business to buy, it's important to conduct a thorough, objective investigation.

You will need professional help in buying a franchise. Consider hiring an attorney and an accountant. The tax rules surrounding franchises are often complex. A specialist in franchise law can assist you with evaluating the franchise package and tax considerations. An accountant can help you determine the full costs of purchasing and operating the business and even help estimate potential profit.

Before you decide if one of these options is right for you, make sure you know the basics of franchising and buying an existing business. The main difference between franchising and buying an existing business is the level of *control* you'll have over your business.

If you're interested in franchising, you should be obtaining a copy of the following:

> **All existing reports:** To start, get a Uniform Franchise Offering Circular (UFOC) from the franchiser. This form contains vital details about the franchise's legal, financial, and personnel history.
>
> **Associated rules and regulations:** Every franchise is different. Confirm that you'll have the right to use the franchise name, trademark, and do business in an area protected from other franchisees. You can also find out if you'll get training and management help from the franchiser and be able to use the franchiser's expertise in marketing and advertising.
>
> **Contracts:** The contract between the two parties usually benefits the franchiser more than the franchisee. The franchisee generally needs to meet sales quotas and buy equipment, supplies, and inventory. Make sure you understand it all before signing.
>
> **Royalty fees:** A royalty fee is a license agreement by the franchiser for the right to use the franchisers assets. The franchisee pays a monthly fee to the franchiser for this right.

Tax filing deadlines

March 15 – Calendar-year S corporation income tax returns are due.

March 15 – Partnership tax returns are due.

March 15 — Deadline for calendar-year corporations to elect corporation status.

April 15 – Individual income tax returns are due.

April 15 – C corporation income tax returns are due.

April 15 — Deadline for IRA contributions.

April 15 – Deadline for personal income tax extensions.

October 15 – Deadline for filing individual income tax return if you filed an extension.

Record retention for businesses

Accounting records

Expense records . . . . 7 years

Financial statements (annual) . . . . Permanent

Fixed assets . . . . Permanent

General ledger . . . . Permanent

Tax returns . . . . Permanent

Bank Records

Bank statements . . . . 7 years

Cancelled or substitute check . . . . 7 years

Corporate minutes . . . . Permanent

Bylaws . . . . Permanent

Shareholders records . . . . Permanent

Stock registers . . . . Permanent

Employee records

Employment applications . . . . 3 years

Payroll records . . . . 7 years

GOALS

Goals give you direction and purpose.

There is magic in setting and writing down goals. It sets into motion a powerful psychological, spiritual, and emotional force.

When you let yourself become obsessed with a goal, you receive the physical power, energy, and enthusiasm needed to accomplish your goal.

The most amazing thing about a deeply entrenched goal is that it keeps you on course to reach your target. This isn't double-talk. What happens is this. When you surrender to your goal, the goal works itself into your subconscious mind. Your subconscious mind is always in balance. The goal is absorbed into your subconscious mind and you react the right way automatically.

- Turn everything into a goal.
- If you want it, make it a goal.
- Write your goals on paper. There is extraordinary power in jotting down goals.
- Set goals regularly and as needed.
- Check off the goals you reach.
- Be patient.

GOALS

1.

2.

3.

4.

5.

BIBLIOGRAPHY

Tax Cuts and Jobs Act of 2017

U.S. Small Business Administration

The Kiplinger Letter

Business News Daily

Wikipedia.org

Tax Foundation

Internal Revenue Service

The Wall Street Journal